YORKSHIRE MURDER STORIES

A COLLECTION OF SOLVED AND UNSOLVED MURDERS

Stephen Wade

BRADWELL
BOOKS

Published by Bradwell Books

9 Orgreave Close Sheffield S13 9NP

Email: books@bradwellbooks.co.uk

British Library Cataloguing in Publication Data: a catalogue record for this book is available from the British Library.

1st Edition

ISBN: 9781910551196

Print: Gomer Press, Llandysul, Ceredigion SA44 4JL

Design by: Andrew Caffrey

Typeset by: Mark Titterton

Photograph Credits: The Author and credited individually

CONTENTS

INTRODUCTION

In this collection of horrendous transgressions committed in England's largest county, I have assembled tales from across the centuries, from Civil War times to the 1960s. The killers' methods range from poison to shotguns, and from attacks in the dark to cruel murder in broad daylight.

Most of these cases are not famous or infamous, but they all share one feature: the taking of a human life in situations of extreme passion, whether through a desire for profit or from a need to remove the victim from this earth, for some kind of heinous satisfaction.

I have included a number of unsolved cases, and these present a special allure to the general reader as much as to the crime investigator: 'who dunnit' is the key word. This is a notion that moves us to read crime novels and also to feel the unease that a crime scene from long ago seems to have for us.

Overall, the county known as 'Broad Acres' has given the annals of murder some of their most gruesome and puzzling cases. Strangely, when we read these stories today, we find that though contexts change over time, the basic human passions never do, and these may sometimes lead to the killing of another person.

Stephen Wade

A COLONEL IS CUT DOWN

IN WAR, MORALITY IS THROWN OUT OF THE WINDOW AND DOUBLE-DEALING IS THE ORDER OF THE DAY. IN THE ENGLISH CIVIL WAR, WHEN BROTHER FACED BROTHER, THERE WERE MANY TRAPS AND BETRAYALS, AND SOMETIMES EVEN THE TOP MILITARY MEN PAID WITH THEIR LIVES WHEN THEY WERE IN THE WRONG PLACE AT THE WRONG TIME.

On 29 October 1648 Colonel Thomas Rainsborough was in Doncaster, staying in a place that should have been safe for him, yet he was killed by armed men, and history has given us different accounts of that murder. But the most likely seems to be that Rainsborough's captain of the guard was not at his post when a strong party of Royalists rode into town from Pontefract Castle. The captain was, it was said, 'at a whore-house in the town' and three other guards were apparently asleep.

The Royalists arrived at about eight in the morning, and they said that they were there to deliver a letter from Cromwell. We might ask why it would take a party of

An early illustration of Colonel Rainsborough being attacked – The author

over forty men to deliver a letter, but that did not occur to whatever guards were around the place, and the Royalists went into Rainsborough's room. A door had been left open and it was an easy task to grab him, with some of the troops having their pistols drawn. The Colonel was taken downstairs, saying, 'Now, gentlemen, what is your business?'

It seems almost certain that a kidnap was their main intention, but Rainsborough resisted and would not go with them. He said he would rather die there than leave with them. Matters were soon out of hand when the prisoner refused to mount his horse and called for help from a guard who was quite near. The Royalists turned nasty and one man stabbed Rainsborough. He was wounded but wanted to fight on and called for a sword. He was run through his body and one of the attackers shouted for him to be shot. One report says that Rainsborough, though severely wounded, got to his feet as the killers mounted and began to ride off; he shouted at them and they turned back to finish him. It is said that he was then stabbed eight times. A maid in the house heard the Colonel cry out, 'I am betrayed! I am betrayed!' What seems obvious now, with hindsight, is that it was all meant to happen. Not only was the captain of the guard absent and some sentries asleep, but no other men came to his aid, and it is certain that the struggle lasted around ten minutes.

A version told by a Royalist, published a long time after the events, makes sense in that it insists that the plan was to take Rainsborough hostage and keep him at Pontefract. A prominent and popular Royalist leader, Sir Marmaduke Langdale, was a prisoner at Nottingham, and an exchange was intended. Two brothers called Paulden led this enterprise, and this account states that the gang stopped at Mexborough, rested and then sent in a spy to Doncaster to check on the state of affairs with regard to Rainsborough's situation. Then they entered the town under the pretence of being from a regiment led by someone called White and said they had a letter from Cromwell. The Paulden gang told the Colonel that they would not harm him if he went quietly with them. The story went that Rainsborough yelled out 'Arms!' and so a fight started.

This account says that one man from Paulden's group wrestled Rainsborough to the ground, trying to hold him rather than attack or kill him, but then one of Rainsborough's own men came and accidentally stabbed him; this was then followed by a deadly sword wound when it was seen that there was never going to be a hostage. Paulden had split his force of over twenty men into smaller groups and positioned them at strategic points in Doncaster. It was a very well-conceived plan, except for the fact that Rainsborough did not have the temperament to give in and accept his becoming a hostage. The account from Paulden says:

A cornet which was one of our four running after him and not willing to kill him caught him by the waistcoat; and in the struggle Rainsborough got his sword and Rainsborough's lieutenant his pistol but Rainsborough was thrown down and one of our troopers ran him through the throat with his sword…

So one story says that there was an officer trying to defend the colonel, and another that says that Rainsborough simply faced the gang alone and his death warrant was when he screamed out an alarm.

The wider picture at the time is interesting. First, it has to be noted that Rainsborough was a man of the 'left' in the sense that he was a man with what were then called 'leveller' views, and he wanted King Charles I dead and a new society created with more equality. Cromwell took more of a middle position politically, and he had a more extreme pro-King arm represented by Fairfax. In all this political disagreement, it has to be pointed out that there had been an earlier attempt to kill Rainsborough. At that time he was at St Albans, and had just ruthlessly executed two Royalist leaders called Lucas and Lisle. This extremism made him enemies: he only had one captain with him as he rode to London, and three men assaulted him. But Rainsborough and his officer put up a good fight and the would-be killers rode off.

What was the truth of all this, then? Did Cromwell or some other party in the Parliamentarian forces want Rainsborough dead? Or was it just a hostage-taking attempt that went terribly wrong? The historian, Hugh Ross Williamson, says that some interesting information about where Rainsborough was and how he was defended had got into the possession of the assassins, if that is what they were. He was staying at a prominent inn by the marketplace, a tavern run by a man called Mawood. We know that he had told Mawood what his plans were for the day on which he was attacked and killed – and this included the statement, 'I expect order but am uncertain.'

Williamson suggests that the party of Royalists were actually Roundheads in disguise. When they rode off they shouted, 'Farewell Rainsborough, farewell Cavaliers!' He says that they could have shouted that as soon as their disguise did not matter any longer.

Whatever the truth of the whole affair, one thing is certain: Doncaster's marketplace was the scene of a murder – and a significant one. 'It is probable that the murder of Rainsborough changed the course of English history,' says Williamson.

The story, as first told, is the one which has been passed down into popular history. This account was retold in the travel guides and on journeys through Yorkshire in the Victorian and Edwardian years, and as late as 1930, in a book called *Highways and By-Ways of Yorkshire*, the author accepts that there was no assassination attempt – merely a romantic bunch of bold Cavaliers outwitting the Roundheads but bungling the kidnap attempt, and seeing Rainsborough die in an accidental way in the midst of a fight. That particular writer says, 'Thus this bold plot miscarried through the obstinacy of a hot-headed man who… positively would not let himself be kidnapped.' It is hard not to see the murder, however, as a very convenient death for the Cromwell cause.

THE TEACHER TURNS NASTY

SOMETIMES, IN THE CHRONICLES OF CRIME, IT HAPPENS THAT AN UPRIGHT, RESPECTED CITIZEN IS INVOLVED IN SOME NEFARIOUS ACT – EVEN MURDER. SUCH AN EVENT COMES AS A TERRIBLE SHOCK TO THE LOCAL TOWNSFOLK, AND SUCH WAS THE INFAMOUS CASE OF EUGENE ARAM, A MAN WHOSE LIFE CAPTURED THE IMAGINATION OF GENERATIONS THAT CAME LONG AFTER HIS TIME.

The story of schoolmaster Eugene Aram and a strange death in Knaresborough is arguably Yorkshire's most mysterious unsolved case of murder. That may seem an odd thing to say, given that Aram was sentenced for the murder of Daniel Clark and subsequently hanged, but the truth is that there are several doubts about Aram's guilt. It is tempting to suggest that enemies wanted him charged and out of the way; after all, a former friend gave evidence against him, and that evidence clearly made the man, Houseman, an accessory.

Aram was born in Netherdale in 1704 and was something of a prodigy of self-education. His father was a gardener, but Aram was clearly destined for a career in the field of learning and education; he spent some time in London as a bookkeeper and then came home to Knaresborough in 1734, where he gained some experience as a tutor. Later he became a schoolmaster and moved to Lynn in Norfolk. We are asked to believe that a learned gentleman with a good income would mix with people of disreputable character, because a murder was committed sometime within the period between Aram being employed in Knaresborough in 1734 and the finding of a body in 1758. In that year a labourer digging ground to make a lime-kiln at Thistle Hill found a human skeleton. At the coroner's inquest, someone stated that, fourteen years before, a man called Daniel Clark had disappeared without a trace. The names of Aram and Houseman were linked to Clark, as they had been friendly at the time.

That is where the drama of this case began: Aram was traced to Lynn and arrested, then brought back to Yorkshire for trial at the York Assizes. But all that has been written about the alleged murder since then has focused on the crucially important questions such as whose body was it that had been discovered? There was no proof it was Clark's. Also, the testimony of Houseman, who was the main witness called against Aram at York, was clearly biased and untrustworthy. In addition, much of the evidence was all circumstantial. But perhaps most remarkable of all was the fact that Aram conducted his own defence.

At that time (and not until 1896) the accused could not speak except in response to the judge's call for 'anything to say' at the end of the trial and before sentence was passed. But Aram acted for himself and did a thoroughly efficient job of it. The narrative that emerged about Aram as he was in 1734 is one that suggests Aram, Clark and Houseman were often together; that Aram's marriage had been a failure and his wife had become an implacable enemy against her former husband. These factors became part of the tale of guilt put together by Houseman. He claimed that the three men had exploited the fact that Clark had 'come into money' when he married; valuables were gathered on credit, based on his wife's income (so Houseman said). Then the thieves fell out, and Houseman claimed that he had seen Aram batter Clarke to death in a field as they walked in front of him, one February evening. Aram argued that Houseman would not have been behind them but walking with them, on the way to an important meeting, and also that on a dark February evening he would not have been able to see such a thing. Another important detail was that Aram had had a very serious illness at that time, one which had left his face scarred and his whole constitution weakened.

The most persuasive reasoning in Aram's own defence covered such things as his lack of a motive for doing such an awful deed, and that his basic character and temperament did not fit well with such a murderous act. Aram said of himself: 'Could such a person in this condition take anything into his head so unlikely, so extravagant? I, past the vigour of my age, feeble … with no inducement to engage, no ability to accomplish, no weapon wherewith to perpetrate such a fact; without interest, without power, without motive, without means…'

He also overthrew whatever medical and forensic details might have been deduced from the skeleton. He said that it could have been anyone, from any time. But all this was of no use. Judge Noel was impressed, but there was no material change in his attitude. Aram was thrown upon the mercy of the court and the jury found him guilty.

In jail at York, he attempted suicide, trying to cut his arm with a razor; yet we have, as Lord Birkenhead pointed out long ago, a mystery in that a second letter alleging to be by Aram was found, and it was one that had clearly been fabricated by someone. We do know that Aram wrote some last words and also a poem. He said, 'Though I am now stained by malevolence and suffer by prejudice, I hope to rise fair and unblemished. My life was not polluted, my morals irreproachable, and my opinions orthodox.'

Eugene Aram was hanged at York on 6 August 1759, in a most pathetic state, mainly through the loss of blood he had suffered; his wrists were bound and bloodstained. The ultimate insult to this man, who may have been a killer but who has never had any solid evidence set against him, was that his body was suspended in chains in Knaresborough forest – a kind of gibbeting done to deter other potential malefactors.

An interesting coda to the story is that in 1837 a woman who was living in an almshouse at Wisbech told a writer for *The Gentleman's Magazine* that she had been a girl when Aram was arrested at Lynn and she saw him at the time. She said that the boys of the school had been in tears at the arrest, so much was Aram esteemed by them. The most interesting note from her memory was that she said Aram turned bodily when looking behind him – never merely turning his head. The writer in 1890 who recorded this, added, 'Has any poet, any observer of nature, ever depicted this instance of fear mustering up resolution?' The writer, R.V. Taylor, appears to be trying to suggest that Aram exhibited some kind of possible guilt and fear. As with everything connected with this tragic tale, the truth will never be out.

Aram's poem has some of the most stoical and impressive lines ever written from the death cell:

Calm and compose, my soul her journey takes,

No guilt that troubles, and no heart that aches.

Adieu thou Sun; all bright like her arise;

Adieu fair friends, and all that's good and wise.

A CASE OF PETTY TREASON

IN THE YEARS BEFORE QUEEN VICTORIA'S REIGN BEGAN, THE GOVERNMENT'S ATTITUDE TO SERIOUS CRIME WAS OFTEN BARBARIC IN THE EXTREME. THROUGHOUT THE EIGHTEENTH CENTURY, COUNTLESS THIEVES WERE TRANSPORTED TO THE COLONIES, AND FOR MURDER MANY WERE HANGED. BUT A TRULY HORRENDOUS FATE AWAITED A WIFE WHO TOOK THE LIFE OF HER HUSBAND. THIS IS THE SAD TALE OF WOMAN, WHO PLOTTED TO TAKE HER MAN'S LIFE.

Over the centuries, York Castle has witnessed some terrible scenes of human suffering, but few can equal the story of Elizabeth Broadingham. The narrative vaguely echoes the actions of Lady Macbeth (lacking the 'milk of human kindness') except that the setting and the motives are the lowest and most despicable imaginable. The tale begins with the notion of the old adage, 'when the cat's away, the mice will play…'

John Broadingham, her husband, was not exactly a pillar of the community. He was locked away in York dungeons for robbery when Elizabeth began her affair

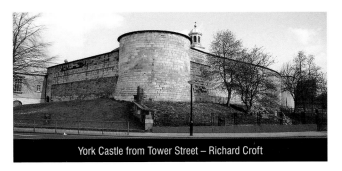
York Castle from Tower Street – Richard Croft

with Thomas Aikney, a man younger than she. It was a case of extreme passion, with her husband out of the way, and she liked the pleasures she found with the other man so much that she moved in with him.

A man coming out of prison after all kinds of deprivations expects some comfort and loyalty from his family. John Broadingham found none of this: he merely found that his wife had left their home. Elizabeth appears to have wanted more than simply living with Aikney as his partner; she wanted to be free of the marriage with John, and to remove the husband from the scene altogether was her aim.

She began to work on Aikney with a view to leading him into the murder of John. The younger man at first resisted these pleas and wiles, but after some time he began to be influenced. It is recounted, though not definitely known, that Elizabeth made sure that Aikney had plenty of alcohol in him and tempted him in all

17

the ways she could invent, as she allured him into a murderous pact. He finally went along with the plan.

Elizabeth must have been a very influential speaker and something of an actress; not only had she inveigled her way into Aikney's life, she now played the part of a good wife, returning to John and apparently wanting to rekindle the marital harmony they had once enjoyed. John took her back. But only a week or so after moving back home, she was talking to Thomas Aikney about their plan, and sorting out the details of where and when it would be done. The lover still vainly tried to resist, but she was relentless. Poor Thomas thought that the best move was to run away and avoid the confrontation, to make a new start elsewhere.

Things came to a head on the night of 8 February 1776 when Elizabeth woke her husband as there was a loud noise downstairs; John staggered down to investigate and made his way to the door, where Aikney was pounding on the wood. As John Broadingham opened up, Aikney knifed him in the chest and then, as the frenzied attack continued, he stabbed the man in the thigh and the leg. With the knife stuck in his belly, John managed to walk out into the street where he was seen by neighbours.

So badly was the husband hurt that he had almost been eviscerated in the assault; he was clutching his stomach and his guts were exposed. The report at the time states that he was 'supporting his bowels'.

John Broadingham died the day after the attack. It took only a short time for neighbours and the magistrate to find Aikney and then the whole story was revealed. Elizabeth and Thomas confessed and he was hanged at York on 20 March. In this tale lies the incredible difference between punishment for murder and petty treason; Aikney's body, as was the custom, was cut down and then transported to Leeds Infirmary for use in dissection work with medical education. But Elizabeth had committed petty treason. Her fate was to be burnt at the stake. The only humane act in these cases was that the executioner normally strangled the woman before the fire was set alight, and he did so for Elizabeth. She was burnt, and some ghoulish witnesses collected her ashes as souvenirs.

Mercy never entered into the matter when a woman was considered for the death penalty in the late eighteenth and early nineteenth century. The great journalist of the period, J.W. Robertson Scott, has a memory of a woman on a scaffold at this time: '… *it was an old woman, a mere old wrinkled, wretched bundle. She was said to have killed a bastard. She cried, "You cannot hang me!" But they did.*'

Burning for petty treason was abolished in 1790: but that was too late for Elizabeth Broadingham.

POISON DID THE TRICK

SOME MURDER CASES IN HISTORY STAND OUT AS PARTICULARLY NASTY – THE PRODUCT OF A CRUEL, DEVIOUS MIND. IN THIS INSTANCE, BACK IN THE GEORGIAN YEARS, WE HAVE THE TALE OF A WOMAN WHO BECAME KNOWN AS 'THE YORKSHIRE WITCH'. SHE APPEARS TO HAVE TAKEN LIVES SIMPLY FOR FINANCIAL GAIN, AND HER CHOSEN METHOD OF SEEING OFF HER VICTIMS WAS POISON.

The criminal justice system that operated in Georgian times was so repressive and extreme that offences were treated harshly primarily on the assumption that the fear of the consequences would reduce crime. The facts say otherwise, and there are numerous infamous murder cases from that period; this is one of them.

At five o'clock on a chill Monday morning in March 1809, 41-year-old Mary Bateman was brought from her cell in York to keep her date with the hangman. Knowing that pregnant women were spared the noose, she had tried to 'plead her belly' to save her neck, but it was no use. A massive crowd had gathered; they wanted their entertainment and to see justice done.

What had she done, this woman from Asenby near Thirsk, to come to such a sorrowful end? The jury were in no doubt that she had poisoned Rebecca Perigo of Bramley, near Leeds. Her crime had been carried out in such a protracted and cunningly planned way that her evil was seen to be more outrageous and callous than many another poisoning case of the time. Mary had schemed to defraud Perigo, and when she was apprehended was clearly aiming to poison another victim who suspected her of the crime. When arrested, a phial of deadly poison was found on her. This had happened in 1806, when apparently Mrs Perigo had suddenly been taken ill with a seizure (a 'flacking' in the local dialect) and collapsed. It was generally held that some evil curse had been put on her.

Bateman had developed into a controlling force on the Perigos, and she sent them pudding and honey; these were to be the means of poisoning. The *Newgate Calendar* states that 'the most important testimony was that of Mr Chorley the surgeon, who distinctly proved that he had analysed what remained of the pudding and of the honey pot, and that he found them both to contain a deadly poison called corrosive spirit of mercury…'

If the cause of death was indeed mercury poisoning, then the stuff would have had to be well saturated in the food, because mercury gives off a very toxic vapour. The substance probably used here was mercuric chloride, a corrosive which in an amount of fifteen grains would bring about heart failure, with horrible burning of the mouth and stomach in the initial period after consumption.

Mary was said to have been a nasty piece of work from her youth; according to the *Newgate Calendar*, 'Within two months of her marriage she was found to have been guilty of many frauds', and that source also says that it was in 1799 that she moved to live in Marsh Lane, Leeds, to 'deal in fortune telling and the sale of charms'.

Her offences were seen as even more devious and damnable when it was learned that she had attempted to practise witchcraft even while in prison. She had extorted money from a young girl who wanted to see her sweetheart, by sewing a charm and coins into her dress: a charm that would, she claimed, mysteriously force the young man she loved to come and visit her in the jail. Naturally, when it didn't work, the material was torn open and the coins were gone – into Mary's pocket. There had been plenty of other 'cunning folk' around the Leeds area, and it is useful here to bear in mind just how popular they were, so we can understand Bateman's success.

An early engraving of Mary Bateman – The Author

At the trial, when Mary claimed she was pregnant, the scene almost dissolved from solemnity into farce. The judge wanted a group of matrons in the court to examine Mary to prove her condition and, as no one wisely wanted to be involved in this, the good ladies of York began to shuffle out of the courtroom with some indignation. But the law prevailed. The judge ordered the doors to be shut so that the women had no choice but to comply and Mary was duly inspected, pronounced to not be with child, and so the sentence was passed. The trial had lasted for eleven hours.

The jailer, who was with her on her last night, noted that she wrote a letter to her husband and sent her wedding ring home to be given to her daughter. She had her youngest child in the cell with her, to suckle, and it was a scene that the Ordinary (the officer who normally interviewed and monitored statements by prisoners) noted with feelings of sympathy. However, he also remarked on her silence regarding the crimes she had committed – and felt sure that she knew much more about other suspicious deaths connected with her activities. In the end, these secrets went to the grave with her.

At this time, notable killers and footpads attracted great crowds at their death, and Mary Bateman was no exception. Though there were no friends to swing on her legs and quicken her death, there was, nevertheless, a crowd to prove her status as a dubious celebrity. A massive crowd had travelled from Leeds, where she had committed murder, to see justice done. The hanging took place at the new drop, behind the Castle. It was eerily quiet when Mary said a prayer, but a shudder went through the crowd when she begged for mercy and shouted that she was innocent.

Her body was taken away to be used for medical dissection, all the way to Leeds by hearse. But, as with all celebrities, her death provoked a general curiosity to view the body and Mary's was no exception. So many people came to look at her corpse that the money raised from this was £80 and 14 shillings – a great deal of money then. It was given to the general infirmary. This was all due to the opportunism of the enterprising William Hey, who saw the chance for some easy fund-raising.

Mary Bateman figured prominently in the *Newgate Calendar* in the 1820 period of its issue. It appears that she was full of tricks and cons, even on one occasion having a hen appear to lay an egg with 'Christ is Coming' written on the shell. So she became the stuff of myth and tall tales. After all, this was the time when 'Old Boney' (Napoleon Bonaparte) would reputedly come and get naughty children. Maybe others were threatened with a visit from the restless spirit of Mary the Poisoner.

One macabre coda to her story is that, in *Yorkshire Notes and Queries* for 1891, the editor notes that 'The tongue of Mary Bateman is in the possession of a gentleman in Ilkley, with whom we are personally acquainted. There is absolutely no doubt as to its genuineness. The curious reader may see it at any time by the courtesy of the present owner.'

MURDER OF A WIFE

IN THE HISTORY OF MURDER THERE ARE SOMETIMES INTERESTING FOOTNOTES TO THE ACTUAL STORY OF THE KILLING. THIS MAY BE, AS IN THE STORY OF CAPTAIN SLACK, WHEN A COMMON KILLER MEETS A MUCH MORE FAMOUS MAN – IN THIS CASE, IN THE CELLS OF DARTMOOR PRISON.

On 11 July 1867 around six o'clock, Thomas Slack, aged forty, came home from a long drinking session; he found his wife, Ann, also drunk. They lived at the Holmes in Wheatley. A little girl had been helping Ann do some housework, and she had left just before Thomas appeared on the scene. The house had a kitchen and a front room, and later it was ascertained where exactly Slack struck – for he did strike, just minutes after coming home. He went into a rage upon seeing her drunk; he took out his pocket knife and stabbed her in the neck. Ann staggered outside, screaming for help. She was bleeding heavily, of course, and she fell as she went outside, into the arms of a neighbour who had rushed to the spot.

The woman who first held the dying woman was Hannah Slack (aunt by marriage to the prisoner) and she left Ann, breathing her last, with another woman before going inside and confronting the man. Hannah found him in the front room sitting on a sofa with his hand in his pocket and she said, 'You have murdered your wife!'

Slack answered, 'I have not seen her, where is she?' But the drunk strangely then added, 'Oh is she dead? She was my best friend… I'm very sorry.'

Hannah Slack now emerges as the heroine in the tale. The hand in his pocket grasped his knife and he said that he was going to take his own life. Hannah restrained him and shouted for help. It was very risky for her to have gone in there alone in the first place. The other neighbours around responded and came to her assistance. Slack was grabbed and held, and a short time after the police arrived, led by Superintendent Astwood, who arrested Slack and took him away. He was charged with murder but he was sober enough to say that it was not so, because he was in drink. That was significant, because at court he stood indicted on charges of both murder and manslaughter.

The definition of murder needs to be stated at this point in the sad story: a murder is a killing which is done 'with malice aforethought' – there has to be a *mens rea* – the aim to kill – and then the *actus reus* – the deed done which would lead to the taking of life. The two Latin terms are crucially important. Slack had immediately thought that his drunkenness would be a defence and would pre-empt a murder charge. He was wrong.

Dr Charles Fenton gave medical evidence, saying he arrived on the scene about forty-five minutes after the deadly attack. He found wounds two inches long on Ann's neck; this was close to the left ear and death had been caused by the piercing of the carotid artery. It was clear from this that the knife wound had caused the death.

It was looking bleak for Slack. His defence, Mr Price QC, introduced the notion of provocation, saying, 'I have known and worked with the family for several years… Mr Slack is a good and kind husband. The deceased was very unkind and provoking in every sense of the word. She did not bear a good character.'

Price then launched into the high drama of the plea aimed at the jury, insisting that this had not been wilful murder. He said, cleverly, that the law was bound to lay down general principles, but the application of these principles lay with the jury. In other words, he was angling for the charge of wilful murder to be dropped by reason of severe provocation. The argument was that Slack had suffered long and hard over the years, worthily trying to bring this fallen woman back to habits of sobriety.

But Hannah Slack's testimony was crucially important. Slack had some barges on the River Don, hence his nickname, 'Captain' Slack, and Hannah pointed out that he was often away from home; their marriage was a very unhappy one, she said. Then she described how she had seen both of them very drunk on that fateful evening. After the killing but before Hannah had known about it, she saw Slack walking along the garden and he 'doubled up his hands and ruffled his hair in quite a delirious manner.'

Price was stretching all sinews and brain cells to paint a good picture of Slack. He cross-examined Hannah and she explained, 'He has had to call me up dozens of times when he could not get the deceased to bed because she was so drunk… I have often seen men come to the house when he has been away.' The tale of their life together was depressing. Hannah pointed out that when the Slacks were first married they had a well-furnished house. Drink had led Ann to pawn absolutely everything for beer or gin-money, and Hannah pointed out that there was not even a blanket in the house to put over the dead body.

It was seeming that the man had been driven to distraction, and the presiding judge, Mr Justice Lowe, asked Price if he intended to set up an insanity defence. The answer was no: he was keeping to the provocation appeal.

The Slacks had been married for ten years, but for the last six months the decline had been extreme. Hannah said that Slack had been going to Sheffield almost every day in that period, and coming home drunk, finding yet more items pawned, and both of them heading for complete destitution.

There was no doubt about the version of events given at the first statement: Mary Humphrey, a neighbour, testified that she had held Ann as she died, and confirmed that she was very intoxicated. Thomas Bramworth, another neighbour, came to the scene and he recalled saying, 'Slack, whatever have you done?' and the man had replied, 'Do save her life and take mine... she was the best friend I had!'

Superintendent Astwood confirmed that Slack had denied murder when in custody in Doncaster. So what was the situation at that point? It was that Slack was being painted for the jury as a man distracted, one who, although he had a severe drink problem himself, was possibly stretched to mental instability all because of his wife. In other words, there was no talk of his actions causing the relationship to deteriorate and no account of his failure to act with regard to the financial worries – all he had done was spend more.

The jury found Slack guilty of manslaughter. But the judge had a shock in store for Slack and for Price, his barrister. He summed up with an oblique and vague reference to potential human understanding of Slack's situation, saying, 'I am quite sure that both the jury and myself would gladly give effect to any circumstances if they could do so consistently with their duty.' But there was a word from his mouth that had a tone of foreboding for Slack: he said 'But…'.

His final words were: 'The jury has taken a very merciful view of this case. There was no doubt that it was a moral murder, although legally manslaughter. If any circumstances should arise, either as regarded his health or otherwise, they must be the subject of an application to a higher authority. But I feel it right, for an offence of this kind, although committed in a moment of drunkenness and repented afterwards, to have a sentence of twenty years' penal servitude.'

This was a bombshell in the court. The sentence was, in those times, virtually a sentence to a future of a 'living death.' Slack would enter a limbo in which he would move from hard labour and fearful discipline into such a drain of his self-identity that should he live to the age of sixty and complete the sentence, he would be a broken man.

Dartmoor Prison – iStock

That living death had a famous witness. Irish radical Michael Davitt was serving his time in Dartmoor when Slack crossed his path. Davitt describes Slack as the very epitome of the prisoner who manages to keep some hope in his mind, and even after serving twelve of his twenty years, Slack tells Davitt, 'I am certain the Secretary of State will discharge me.' How wrong can a man be? But the fact that the two men met is a special case: such encounters are almost never on record anywhere – the political prisoner of great fame meeting the common murderer and thinking it worth recording.

BILL O'JACKS

YORKSHIRE HAD ITS STRETCHES OF WILDERNESS BACK IN VICTORIAN TIMES. ONE OF THE MOST LAWLESS PARTS OF THE COUNTY BACK THEN WAS IN THE WASTES OF SADDLEWORTH MOOR, LATER NOTORIOUS FOR ITS CONNECTION WITH THE CRIMES OF BRADY AND HINDLEY. IN 1832, A DARK YEAR FOR THE NORTH, AS CHOLERA RAGED THROUGH MANY TOWNS AND DISCONTENT RAVAGED THE RURAL AREAS, A CRUEL MURDER, UNSOLVED TO THIS DAY, WAS PERPETRATED ON THESE ISOLATED MOORS.

Arguably, this is the most sensational and dramatic unsolved Yorkshire murder ever perpetrated. Known also as the Moorcock Inn case or the Marsden Moor murders, this is the tragic tale of a double murder at the lonely inn on Marsden Moor in 1832 in which several facts and clues seem to have a definite bearing on the resolution, but eventually come to nothing.

Bill O'Jacks on Saddleworth Moor – The author

The victims were 84-year-old William Bradbury, landlord of the inn (known as Bill O'Jacks) and his son Thomas, aged 46. They had been shot and there had been a massive struggle, as Thomas was a giant of a man who was in the habit of throwing nuisance drinkers over the back wall. This strongly built, powerful man was shot along with his father, Bill, who before he died made the intriguing statement that 'Pat' or 'Pad' – the dying man's voice was indistinct – did the deed. Now, the complication comes in the detail that there were Irish workers nearby (known as 'paddies') and also that there were local pedlars near called Burn Platters. A man called Reuben Platt had listened to the old man foolishly talk about his stash of money in the bar, and he was suspected. But there was a major suspect in the person of Red Bradbury, from a local criminal family. His brother Tom had been prosecuted for poaching by the Bradbury family who owned the pub (they were not related) and was due to appear in court in Pontefract the day after the murder.

William, living in such a rural spot, without immediate sources of help, had foolishly bragged about his fear of banks, and his habit of keeping money on the premises. There is no doubt that he was inviting trouble. The temptation of such an invitation to rob him was too much for someone who had listened and made a decision to do anything that might be required in order to take that stash of cash. The murder scene was horrendous. Poor Mary, the old man's granddaughter, walked in on a scene of carnage. The big man had obviously fought for his life, and the room was wrecked.

Until the time that the Moorcock was pulled down in 1937, the murder and the surrounding area became the subject of morbid tourism and local folklore, with ghost stories attached to the tale as well. The best guide to this impact is perhaps the text on the tombstone of the victims in Saddleworth churchyard:

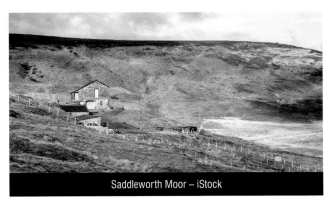
Saddleworth Moor – iStock

Those who now talk of far-famed Greenfield's hills,
Will think of Bill o' Jacks and Tom o' Bills,
Such interest did their tragic end excite,
That 'ere they were removed from human sight,
Thousands on thousands daily came to see
The bloody scene of the catastrophe.

There are several nasty aspects to this killing. For a start, one of the victims was vulnerable in the extreme – William being in his eighties – and the other was so large and strong that he had to be cut down by a number of assailants, and had been clubbed and stabbed to death. These facts, along with the wild nature of the setting, well away from any settled community with its networks of friendship and support, has made the story a compelling one. From time to time, interested parties look again into the horrible events of that day, as in 1959, when the Saddleworth History Club resolved to investigate. They had at least six suspects to work on, and they tried hard to create a scenario that would lead to some kind of explanation, but they hit a brick wall, as so often happens in the scrutiny of cold cases from so long ago, in the mists of provincial history.

HURLED TO HER DEATH

IN DESPERATE TIMES, PEOPLE MAY RESORT TO WORK THAT CAN ENDANGER THEIR VERY LIVES. IN THE DAYS BEFORE THE WELFARE STATE, POOR FOLK HAD TO RESORT TO SUCH EXTREME MEASURES AS WHAT WE NOW CALL THE SEX INDUSTRY, EXCEPT THAT, IN THE MENACING AND VULNERABLE STREETS OF VICTORIAN BRADFORD, THERE WAS NO 'TEAM' OR ANY KIND OF SUPPORT, AND THE WORST COULD HAPPEN TO A WOMAN ALONE.

There are murders that show mankind at its very worst, the lowest level of moral degradation to which people can sink, and this Bradford case is just such a tale.

When we examine the lives of prostitutes in the Victorian period, the extent of the risks they ran in their everyday lives is truly remarkable and often incredibly reckless and wrong-headed. In their trade they had to inhabit not only the dark world of the industrial city on a smoggy evening, among beer-shops and inns, but in the daylight, when there was still custom, they adapted and tried to survive. Many failed, and such a one was Liz Shepherd. At just 28 years old, she was working at any time when there might be clients, and her need for strong drink led to her death.

At three o'clock one morning in May 1871, Liz fell from a high building at the junction of Manchester Road and Little Horton Lane. It was a quick death, as she slammed onto the ground and fractured her skull. Around midnight the night before, she had taken up with three young men, and one of them had suggested that they all go up to his workshop, a room on a very high level, and accessed by a long and cramped circular spiral staircase. They had planned a night of debauchery, and carried a gallon of beer and a bottle of whisky with them, as one man, called Barraclough, said that the workshop would be a quiet and private place in which to enjoy themselves. He had the keys to the place, as he had formerly been employed as a wire-worker there.

The group, comprising Liz, Barraclough, Richard Gray and Harry Harte, soon felt the effects of the alcohol and things got out of hand. They had met Liz at the Queen's Hotel and knew her reputation. This was that she wasn't too choosy about the company she kept, and that when plied with liquor she was good entertainment. But the party became noisy, and a police officer called Bower, on

An early illustration of Liz Shepherd falling to her death – The author

his beat in the area, reached the yard near the base of the building and heard an altercation. A woman's voice screamed out something, and a man's voice in reply said, 'Make less noise or I'll fettle your canister for you.' In the dialect of the time, it was an expressive way to threaten extreme injury.

Other constables were called, but none could trace the place where this was coming from, and after some time more shouts were heard. This time, PC Bower heard a call of 'Mr Smith' and 'Police!' Looking up, he saw the figure of a woman walking on a high roof. Bower saw Liz roll from the high roof to a lower one, then scramble a little before she lost her grip and fell down to her death.

The medical examination was done by Dr Leason, and he testified in court that Liz had several bruises which had been caused by being beaten by fists. It became clear, when the room and landing where the group had been were examined, that the woman had been attacked, and had then struggled and broken free. There were bloodstains on walls and on the stairs. Statements made about the medical examinations revealed the sad and desperate life Liz was leading. She had a few pence stitched into her stocking, and a witness had said that when the deceased had left her lodgings on the morning of the day she died, she had only a penny on her.

Liz had been with Gray when the argument began, and it had been a sordid and nasty row over the cost of her services; a familiar scenario in the lives of these unfortunate women. She had broken away and taken the only exit to freedom that seemed open to her. The point in court was whether or not Gray was guilty of wilful murder? The jury found that he was. He was destined for the next assizes and a death sentence.

It was a heavy day for the women of Liz Shepherd's trade: as if this horrendous assault was not enough, there was a suicide at the same time, a poor woman who had hanged herself. It had only taken fifteen inches of rope fixed on a bedroom cornice to end the life of poor Rebecca Burgin. The coroner's inquest, held at the Northumberland Arms, was assured that there was no other factor in the death: it was an uncomplicated self-murder.

These cases highlight the perilous lives of the oldest profession, and Bradford had had its share of these women for some time. At the very same time as this murder took place, William Logan was writing his book, *The Great Social Evil*, and he noted about Bradford:

The Chief Constable for Bradford, in his report of 1851, that the number of known brothels within the borough was forty two; the number of known prostitutes residing in them was 109; the number of these residing in thirteen beerhouses in the borough, twenty-one – total 130.

Almost every week in the press reports throughout the nineteenth century, there was some woman being attacked while in the course of her professional work. In Liz Shepherd's case, she did not even have a 'minder' and worked alone.

A DESPERATE DUO

WHAT OFTEN STANDS OUT AS OF SPECIAL INTEREST WHEN WE TRY TO UNDERSTAND WHY PEOPLE TAKE OTHERS' LIVES IS THE 'DOUBLE ACTS' – THE COLLABORATION IN A KILLING WHICH HAPPENS ONLY RARELY IN MURDER STORIES. THIS BARNSLEY TALE INVOLVES SUCH A LETHAL COMBINATION.

William and Emily Swann lived in George Square, Wombwell, and they were in the habit of taking in lodgers. When John Gallagher arrived he and Emily became fond of each other and an affair began. When William Swann found out he reacted by throwing Gallagher out. But the lovers continued to see each other. On 5 June 1903, Gallagher had come back to visit Emily, so obviously there would be friction, and William Swann was his usual truculent self. Gallagher, small though he was, made it clear that if Swann harmed Emily, he would come looking for him.

That happened sooner than any of them must have thought. In fact the very next day the lovers met in the home of a Mrs Ward, and, after they had talked a while, Emily went home. But soon she was back, and the first act of the tragedy was to begin. She was badly bruised and had black eyes. As soon as she said, 'See what our Bill has done!' it was the trigger for Gallagher to act. He left, swearing to punish the husband for what he had done.

From that point things got out of hand. Though Gallagher was only slight and lightly built he was handy with his fists and a titanic struggle followed in the Swann house. The fight was so loud and public that neighbours heard and saw things that would later be very important evidence. The most striking statement overheard was Emily shouting, 'Give it to him, Johnny, punch him to death!'

When the first confrontation petered out, Gallagher returned to Mrs Ward's house and started to report that he had broken some of Swann's ribs. He said that he would 'go and give him something for himself for that'. This kind of aggression had been going on for some time, and this day was going to be the end of it. Gallagher said that he had 'busted four ribs and that he would go bust some more'. There were a number of witnesses, to all this trouble.

For a while, since leaving the Swanns, Gallagher had been planning to go to Bradford, and on this day he said, in Ward's home, 'I'll finish him out before I go to Bradford.'

There was a clear intention to kill in that statement, and he was also heard to say, 'I'll murder the pig before morning. If he can't kick a man he shan't kick a woman!' The fight went on in George Square and again Emily's voice was again heard, saying, 'Give it to him, Johnny.'

The end of this battle indoors was that the lovers emerged from her home, hand in hand, and a bystander said that they stood 'with every sign of affection.' There had been over ten minutes of fighting and screaming. Over the years, Emily had often been beaten by William, and that moment when she and her lover came out of the door was surely a moment of freedom for her, whatever the circumstances. The circumstances were that in the house behind them, William Swann lay dead.

It didn't take long for the police to be called, but Gallagher escaped and took to the open road, leaving Emily to face the music. She was arrested but Gallagher was on the loose for months, eventually being found in Middlesbrough.

The two defendants stood together in Leeds on 9 December 1903 before Mr Justice Darling, a man who had been involved in the trial of Oscar Wilde and who was to try, only a few weeks after this, the 'baby farmers' Sach and Walters. The only flimsy shred of an argument for Gallagher was that he had been drinking on the day he killed, and of course that his motives were a reprisal, a strong urge to administer some 'justice' of his own. In the events of that day, inside the home, there had undoubtedly been incitement to kill, and Darling knew this. He said to Emily, 'As for the woman, it is my duty to tell you that one does not commit murder only with one's hands. If one person instigates another to commit murder, and that person does it, the instigator is also guilty of murder.'

It took only half an hour for the jury to find both of them guilty of wilful murder. But there was a strange twist to this tale, because there was a vital piece of evidence which Darling did not mention before the jury retired. It turned out that Emily's part in the killing was far more than incitement. Gallagher had said, after being arrested, that Emily had used a poker to hit her husband and that Gallagher did not touch the dead man. Did this mean that Emily hit her husband after he was dead? All that mattered was that Justice Darling believed her to have been actively involved to the killing of William Swann.

The fact that the verdict was decided without a report of what Gallagher had said about the poker has to say something significant about the feeling concerning Emily's state of mind at the time. After all, people had heard her say that Johnny should kill her husband, and that was all that was required to convince the twelve 'good and true men' in Leeds that day.

But there is another perspective on Emily Swann, one of understanding and compassion, and paradoxically, this comes substantially from the man who hanged her: John Ellis. The bare facts of Emily's fate were given in *The Times* of 29 December 1903:

The Wombwell Murderers – The Home Secretary has declined to interfere in the case of the Wombwell murderers, Emily Swann and John Gallagher, who were found guilty at Leeds Assizes of the wilful murder of the female prisoner's husband. They will be executed at 9 o'clock this morning.

But Ellis is the man who saw the woman inside that apparently murderous beast who broke the laws of nature. He saw a 42-year-old woman, 'a little, stumpy, round-faced woman, only 4 feet 10 inches tall and 122 lbs in weight. She was the first condemned woman I had ever seen, and frankly I didn't think the authorities would allow her to go to the scaffold.' He was wrong, and it affected him greatly.

The couple were told that the reprieve had been dismissed and from that moment, Ellis saw a woman who was emotionally wrecked. Ellis says, 'When she was told of the Home Office decision it absolutely staggered her, and she wore a look of utter misery when I peeped in at her that evening.'

Drawing of hangman John Ellis – The author

The reality Ellis saw was a tiny woman, one who had had to suffer violence for years; she had been beaten, shouted at, despised and humiliated, and now after finding that there had been an opportunity for sheer animal revenge, a momentary release of hatred, as a mad dog would turn on its master after being kicked and beaten, she had become again a small, weak woman, being asked to accept the reality that someone was going to hang her, inside a miserable jail.

Ellis's tone is one of gentleness and as we read his memoir we notice how observant he was – how he saw the wardresses becoming friendly to their female charge and how both prisoners showed 'religious penitence'.

The hangman's account of the deaths of the two lovers is painful reading, as Gallagher was first to the scaffold after being pinioned and then a white hood was placed over his head, so he had no idea that Emily came to stand behind him. She simply said, 'Good morning, John.' He was shocked and replied, 'Good morning, love.'

As the rope was put around the woman's neck she said, plainly, 'Goodbye. God bless you!' According to Ellis, she had gone from being a squirming emotional wreck on the floor of her cell to someone quite stoical, and a glass of brandy was all it took. Her two wardresses had broken down and were very upset, just as Emily bucked up and gave a smile of acceptance of her situation.

BARNSLEY BAD LAD

THE PUBLIC HANGMAN IN VICTORIAN TIMES WAS NOT ALWAYS A POPULAR FIGURE IN SOME PARTS OF THE LAND, IN SPITE OF HIS DARK NATIONAL CELEBRITY. IN THOSE COMMUNITIES IN WHICH HE HAD 'TOPPED' A LOCAL, HIS NAME WAS MORE THAN MUD – IT WAS REVILED AND HATED, AND SOMETIMES THERE WERE THREATS AGAINST HIM, AS WAS THE CASE IN THIS SOUTH YORKSHIRE TALE.

We know a lot about the last days of James Murphy in York before he was hanged, because the hangman, James Berry, kept a journal and published his memoirs. He even managed to joke about his impending death. Accounts of his life and deeds were printed in papers and in the so-called 'penny dreadfuls' – the forerunners of our 'true crime' magazines on the shelves of newsagents today, and immensely popular. It was a story that appealed to many thousands of readers, because it involved poaching, and that method of feeding a starving family, or of earning some beer-money, was indulged in by many, from Cornwall to Orkney.

In some cases, poaching really had been the only resource available to families in order to stave off starvation. If the breadwinner of the family lost his job, or if food was too dear to buy, then survival depended on what could be gleaned for free, from the fields and woods. Poaching was therefore, through the centuries in English everyday history, seen as a 'social crime' – that is, it was committed out of necessity, and so was a special case, when compared to robbery on the highway or to burglary.

Murphy, from Barnsley, was a collier from Lambert's Fold, Dodworth and he had twenty-five convictions for poaching. Murphy, full of vengeance, set out one day to look for a police officer called Austwick, and he shot the man dead. He was cornered and arrested in Barnsley, but there was a local groundswell of feeling that he did not deserve to hang, as it was thought that the crime was done on the spur of the moment, and not premeditated. However, an appeal for a reprieve failed.

The problem for those aggrieved locals was of course that Murphy had deliberately set out to look for the officer. There was no denying the hard fact that the man had a firm intention to either seriously harm, or to take the life of, another person. Any argument for the defence was going to be very slender and ineffective. Murphy was a doomed man, and he must have known it as he brooded in his cell.

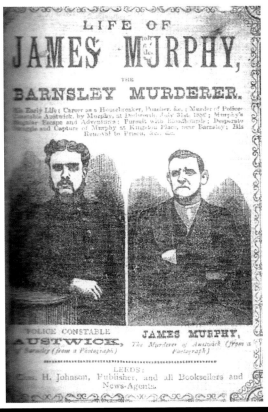

The cover of a book about John Murphy – The author

When Berry came to have his chat in the condemned cell, Murphy said he would not give the hangman any trouble: 'I am not afraid to die. A lot of people have been making a fuss about me. But I'm hanged if I can see what there is to make a fuss about.' Berry was impressed by the sick joke. Murphy had to walk past his own waiting grave on the way to the scaffold and all he said to Berry was that he wanted him to do it 'as painlessly as you can'. The killer was one of the most tough and self-controlled of all Berry's unfortunate clients, and the hangman makes that clear in the way he writes about the melancholy poacher turned police-killer.

Berry's note in his journal was: 'I hanged James Murphy in spite of threats and then I heard that I would never dare set foot in Barnsley, the town whence the victim hailed. People said that the Barnsley miners would murder me, but in spite of the threats I visited the town on many occasions.' Usually, Berry was happy to enjoy his notoriety and the fact that the media took an interest in him. In Leeds, the printer Charles Johnson produced a biography of Murphy in a chapbook, with the title, *The Life of James Murphy the Barnsley Murderer*, and it meant that the killer would be the first name linked to the town in that way. The picture of Murphy on the cover of the book shows a calm, ordinary man with arms folded, as if waiting for a conversation about the weather.

As far as we know, James Berry was never attacked for what he did on that fateful day in the life of the Barnsley bad lad.

A DANGEROUS WOMAN

MURDER AS A RESULT OF THE LUST FOR WEALTH HAS ALWAYS BEEN COMMON IN CRIMINAL HISTORY, AND WHEN MEN COMMIT SUCH DEEDS FOR MONEY, THE VIOLENCE IS OFTEN EXTREME. WOMEN MORE COMMONLY HAVE POISONED THEIR VICTIMS. BUT THIS IS THE STORY OF AN EXCEPTION TO THE RULE.

Lily Waterhouse was 40 years old in 1923, when a woman called Louie Calvert knocked on her door. Lily's husband had died a year before, and she had lived in Amberley Road for fourteen years. She had no idea that Calvert had come to stay with her as part of a ruse to fool her husband. A dangerous woman was on the loose.

Louie had been a housekeeper for a Mr Frobisher the year before this, and that man had been found dead in the River Aire in July 1922. With hindsight it seems peculiar that the coroner did not ask more questions about this corpse. There was a wound on the back of his head and he had no boots on. At the inquest, little Louie appeared and stated that she had pawned the boots for a few shillings. All this was very strange because Frobisher lived a mile or so away from where his body was found. Had he walked barefoot to his death? Was it suicide? It is astounding that the verdict at the inquest was death by misadventure.

That had been the prior appearance of Louie Calvert in the records, but she was destined to become far more prominent than that. She moved on from Frobisher's place to marry Arty Calvert in Hunslet and now here she was, away from home, pretending to be pregnant. She had two children already: one, Kenneth, living with Arty and her; and a girl, Annie, who lived in Dewsbury. So here was a strange situation: a woman of 33 turning up, wanting a room, and then, unknown to the landlady, trying to work out how to get hold of a baby that she could pass off as her own. The obvious thing to do was to advertise, as you would for any goods. The advert in the Leeds paper did indeed work.

A teenager from Pontefract had given birth to a little girl in Leeds and her mother saw Louie's advert. It did not take long to arrange for an adoption; all Louie had to do was lie low in her lodgings and wait until the baby was with her. In this phase of her life we see Louie Calvert the odd performer, acting a role in the community. The situation was extremely bizarre: a married woman living under an assumed identity in another part of the city in which her husband and real home were, pretending to be there in order to care for her newborn, currently in hospital. Yet strangely that would have seemed a plausible tale; at the time many young babies were ill with all kinds of maladies, from diphtheria to scarlet fever.

As if her life were a feature in a B-movie of the time, deception led to more problems in the Waterhouse home. This sprang from the fact that Louie was a compulsive thief, and her pawning of Frobisher's boots had been just one of many visits to the pawnbroker's with items she had stolen. Another startling aspect of Louie Calvert is that, though she was very short and thin, in fact under five feet tall, her personality was forceful and assertive. She was capable of instilling fear in people, using sheer egoistic control and toughness. So much was this evident to Mrs Waterhouse that she was at first frightened to say anything when she began to notice that various objects had disappeared from her home.

But she gathered some determination when she found pawn tickets clearly relating to the objects that had gone missing. This was a time, of course, when many working people were in dire straits and pawning a best Sunday suit almost on a weekly basis was one desperate way of keeping a little ready cash in the house. Louie was reported to the police and sent to court to answer charges, but she returned to her lodgings, packed her bags and her baby, and went home to Calvert's house in Railway Place, Hunslet. As earlier writers on the diminutive Calvert have speculated, how on earth she managed to be so prominent and sociable around Leeds in the time she was supposed to be having a child in Dewsbury is amazing; she was a familiar sight to many, and being distinctive in her build and her speech, she would have been seen by people passing from one area of Leeds to another, perhaps commuting.

It was just before Easter when Louie left the Waterhouse home, and Lily had been seen going into her house the night before Louie was seen leaving; but in those terraces neighbours saw and heard a great deal – there was very little privacy and people were sensitive to any unusual sounds. Domestic arguments would be heard by several neighbours, for instance. On this occasion, a neighbour heard noises in the lodger's room and then saw Louie as she left the house, carrying her baby. She told the neighbour that Lily was upset, but that she (Louie) was going home. She explained the odd noises by lying that she and Lily had been moving a bed.

At last Arty Calvert had his wife back, and also what he thought was his baby, little Dorothy. This was a happy time, of course, and they were up late. But the next morning Arty saw that there was some luggage in the house that had not been there the night before.

Unbelievably, Louie Calvert had returned to Amberley Road in the early hours and had collected this large suitcase; at this stage in her career, Louie was clumsy. She was seen by several people, despite the early time of day, and these sightings would be valuable statements later on in the tale. Even more surprising, as we re-read the case today, is that she left a note. If she had not done that, then the chances are that the dual life she had constructed may well have kept her anonymous when the police started looking for the little woman who had lodged in Amberley Road.

They did indeed start looking for her, very soon after her dawn appearance at the lodgings, and this was because Lily Waterhouse had, of course, started a paper trail for the police when she summonsed her tenant. When Lily did not appear for that, the police came to check on her. What they found in her home was the woman's corpse, lying on the floor in a bedroom; there was plenty of her blood in evidence around the body, even to the extent that some blood had splashed on the wall. She had been battered on the head; there was dried blood clotted on her scalp.

The hallmark was there at the scene, though it was not perceived at the time: Lily Waterhouse was fully dressed – apart from her boots. There had been a violent struggle and the old lady had fought with some tenacity, as she was badly bruised, and it had taken several heavy blows to finish her. It is somewhat difficult to accept, bearing in mind the physical stature of Louie, that Lily Waterhouse had also been strangled. The killer, the police noticed, had cut up cloth to use to tie her hands and feet; yet there must have been something else used to strangle the woman as the ligature marks on her neck were wider than that caused by a strip of cloth. It is a gruesome thought that the noises heard by the neighbours were almost certainly the movements of the dying woman's limbs as she was shaking in her death-throes. Her murderous lodger, small though she was, had been binding her tight, in an effort to stop the noises made by her feet; neighbours would certainly have heard the sounds, and would have come to ask questions. One important detail here is that the room was not carpeted. The sounds of feet thrashing on wooden boards could surely have meant that the murderer would have been disturbed as people responded to the noises heard through paper-thin walls.

What has previously read as the portrait of a widow leading a lonely and rather impoverished lifestyle, as questions were asked in the ensuing investigation, turned out to be something very different. In fact, some of Lily's previous lodgers had been ladies of the night; these were tough times in Leeds and there was high unemployment. A widow with a low income would no doubt have been tempted to take in guests who would pay well, and no questions would be asked. But Lily was also unusual in that she had not been the isolated figure one might have supposed. She had, since her husband's death, had lots of visitors and had lived quite an interesting life, including some dabbling in spiritualism. Neighbours, answering questions about her character, seemed eager to mention the shadier side of Lily's life, even to the point of one commenting that 'She was not a clean woman.'

Understandably, these comments and implications about the victim led to the police trying to look for suspects among the clientele she had mixed with in the recent past. But then people began to recall the lodger with the baby, and there was the matter of the letter Louie had left. It was the letter about the deceit over the birth supposedly in Dewsbury. As this was addressed to Mrs Louise Calvert, there was a lead there. She was soon to be tracked down, and this woman who had been enjoying the strange thrills of moving from one name and identity to another for some time, escaping the reality she perhaps feared, opened her door one night in April 1925 to find Detective Inspector Pass standing there. As has been remarked previously, Louise was an unprepossessing sight, and there was a terrible irony in the fact that one of her assumed names had been Edith Thompson, the name of the celebrated poisoner who had been hanged at Holloway in 1923; for whereas Edith Thompson was sophisticated and articulate, with a real presence, little Louise Calvert was ill-looking, underweight and coarse. Amazingly, Louise was wearing Mrs Waterhouse's boots when she answered the door.

The trial at Leeds was in front of Mr Justice Wright. The court learned that for the two years before she moved in with Calvert, she had lived hand-to-mouth, but had realised that there were ways of exploiting poverty and existing in various roles and guises. Possibly one of the most interesting and informative of these was her time pretending to be in the Salvation Army. Often small details speak volumes and in this case it has to be noted that she had even stolen her bonnet from a proper Salvation Army member. The author of the most exhaustive account of this case has mentioned a neighbour who knew Louise well, and she testified that the little woman had violent tempers, and that she was capable of changing her mood rapidly, and of using bad language. The witness said that the obscenities from Calvert were so extreme that she had banned her from coming into her home.

When Louise Calvert was asked if she had anything to say before the sentence was passed, she said simply, 'Yes, Sir, I'm pregnant.' There is something informative about that statement as it indicates the naive facility she had for a child-like defence when cornered. Saying an infantile thing like that was tantamount to admitting that her sense of reality was very slender and her that inner fantasy, which fed the outer criminal who was a predator in the streets of Leeds, was a truly frightening aspect of her.

As she had constantly avoided making any statements in the witness box with the argument that she was ill –

Leeds Town Hall – iStock

and now supposedly pregnant – a medical inspection was essential. Dr Hoyland Smith went to examine her in the court cell, and as with Mary Bateman, a woman had to attend. She was from a jury of mothers selected for the purpose. But the difficulty was quite in keeping with Calvert's muddled and crazy career: there was no proof either way.

The result was that the death sentence would be passed. A Leeds City Councillor said at the time that he felt pity for her and added, 'She was a thin, wan-looking creature only weighing a few stone. I should never legislate on the lines of hanging a woman.' But others soon realised that there were two Louise Calverts: in the dock she had been quiet, restrained and polite. But down in the cell she shouted abuse at her husband, trying to say that he was to blame. All he could say was, 'It can't be helped, lass.' Other interpretations of her actions and responses to graphic descriptions of the attack on Waterhouse, and of the corpse, indicate that she was unfeeling and mentally distant from any sense of the events unfolding being in any way 'real'.

But the woman who was seen by some as undersized and pathetic had done the awful deed, and she had also been wily and cunning in the extreme. Her actions in court and before the magistrate when first charged show an amount of guile too. She dressed in black and to the local reporters she soon became 'the woman in black'. It has been noted that she fussed over her appearance, as if she were still putting on clothes to be someone else – to project a persona which was not really her. In the magistrates' court, even as evidence was being spoken, she changed her hat, putting on a black silk one instead of her everyday mauve.

There was an appeal. In London, she was again dressed all in black, and the context at the time was a difficult one with regard to the hanging of women; since the notorious Thompson case in 1923, the eight women given a death sentence had all been reprieved. It must have looked too many that this was going to be the case yet again, as a petition had been signed by 3,000 people. Much was made in the press on the topic of her child –

the question of what would happen to it and who might adopt it was something that sold newspapers.

But a factor in the appeal was that she was not pregnant. There was also nothing else that was new. In spite of the media interest in the case and in the very emotive issue of hanging a woman, the sentence was not quashed. The end was in sight for her then; her relatives came to pay a last visit to her in the cell. She actually wrote a letter on her last night on earth and in this she said, 'I am keeping up quite well and you will have the joy of meeting me in heaven, for I am quite ready and prepared to meet my God.'

A MURDEROUS SOLDIER

WARTIME CAN HIDE ANY NUMBER OF VICIOUS CRIMES, AND AN INTENT TO MURDER MAY BE CARRIED OUT IN THE BELIEF THAT THE EVIDENCE WILL BE DESTROYED. BUT THERE WAS NO SUCH THINKING IN THE CASE OF MERVIN MCEWEN, WHO TOOK AN OPPORTUNITY AND MOVED ON, SERIOUSLY UNDER-RATING THE POWER OF GOOD POLICE WORK.

In the Second World War, the incidence of soldiers going on leave and subsequently staying away from their regiment was a common event. Many of them had romantic entanglements; some were sick of the war, and others, like Canadian Mervin McEwen, were adventurers, on the look-out for trouble, and sometimes they found it – in this instance, it was murder.

McEwen settled into an old army hut on Savile Park, Halifax, a place that would later make the national news as the scene of one of the Yorkshire Ripper killings. While there, he chatted to and cultivated local acquaintances, and one such person was an old man called Mark

Left: Moorfield Street Halifax – The author
Right: Savile Park Halifax – Paul Glazzard

Turner, who liked company, and would ask a few men back to his house in Moorfield Street for food and drink. McEwen took up the offer hospitality a few times, and on 2 April 1943 the soldier kept company with the old man.

Turner's absence from the social round was soon noticed and neighbours called the police. The man's body was found, and he had clearly been savagely attacked. The killer, it was noted, was a careless type, having left fingerprints on a whisky bottle. Even more inviting to a detective was the fact that regimental badges and some parts of the uniform of the Royal Canadian Corps were also found in the house in Moorfield Street. The hunt was on – particularly when it was discovered that a soldier had been in the park hut and had recently moved on.

The killer changed his name to Acton and went over the Pennines to Manchester, where he met a woman and planned to begin a new life with a new identity. He must have thought that he had eluded the law, and had taken a life without paying for it. He was wrong – very wrong.

Routine enquiries were being made in McEwen's new neighbourhood, and the killer was to make a fatal mistake. When a police constable knocked on his door, McEwen produced an identity card, which in wartime was essential for every person to have. The problem was that the card was Turner's, and McEwen had stolen it, and then changed the surname to 'Turney'. He was very much under suspicion and had a lot of questions to answer. In fact, he had shown the policeman a picture of the man he had killed.

The account given to the law was that McEwen had gone back to Turner's house, made some food and then imbibed a lot of whisky. In this drunken condition, he had attacked the old man, but he insisted that he had not had any intention of killing him. His argument did not convince the jury at Leeds Assizes and he was sentenced to hang. He left this world in Armley Jail on 3 February 1944.

VIOLET AND WILLIAM

WE KNOW MURDER STORIES SOMETIMES ONLY FROM THE FOOTNOTES, WHEN AN INDIVIDUAL TAKES AN INTEREST IN THE ACCUSED, OR WHEN THERE IS A CRUSADE TO CHANGE THE LAW. SUCH A CASE IS THAT OF THE EPILEPTIC DRIFTER, WILLIAM EDWARDS.

Without the writings of a woman whose life's work is now almost totally forgotten, Violet Van der Elst, this story would not be known about at all. This tireless campaigner for the abolition of hanging wrote about this story: 'His case stands out in my memory, amongst those sad cases I can never forget.' She chose his case for special discussion in her autobiography, a work perhaps most interesting for the photographs of the lady's very large car parked in front of many of the prisons across the land in the 1930s.

On 26 November 1936, William Edwards took the life of the woman he loved. Minutes before her death, she had been weeping for fear of losing him, so much did she love him too. Why Violet Van der Elst found this story a sad case is that the young man had no idea what he had done. He was an epileptic.

Edwards was aged 26 at the time, a man who had been drifting from job to job since leaving school. He had worked at Tankard's Mill in Laisterdyke, at Turners the metal polishers and as a labourer for the Sanda Metal Co. He had been working as a baker's assistant at Newboulds Ltd up to seven weeks before he took Myrtle Parker out for the night. He had known the girl for six months and they had been walking out regularly; he was always at her parents' house in Bierley.

Myrtle was just 20 and worked as a wool spinner; they had met at the Picturedrome in Wakefield Road. They had discussed the possibility of getting married in May and she had agreed to marry him. At that time, she was legally a minor (under 21) so Edwards had to obtain a form of consent from the Marriage Registry Office. He had talked about this with Myrtle's mother and she suggested that they should wait a while. Matters seem to have been good between them; there was no evidence of any acrimony.

On the fatal night the couple walked for about forty minutes and then he left, but they met again at seven that night and after spending some time at her home, they went out and stopped at Merrydale Road. It was there that, as they talked about their future, Myrtle began to weep and, as he later said, 'begged me to stay

Violet Van der Elst – The author

with her'. This upset Edwards and tipped him over into an epileptic fit. He took out his pen-knife and opened it. The report from the trial has this summary of what happened next:

His depression deepened and, as now appears from the reconstruction, he took up the knife and whirled his arm, not knowing where the blow fell. His memory failed him. He has no recollection of what else happened.

Edwards then wandered the streets until he arrived at a friend's house at 5 in the morning and there he slept. But when he woke, he said to his friend, 'I have done my woman in.'

Throughout the nineteenth century there was a continuing debate on what elements of mental illness constituted a defence of insanity and diminished responsibility. In the formative Lincolnshire case of William Drant in the 1870s, the psychologist Henry Maudsley entered the debate about a man who had killed a village constable and had a death sentence was reprieved, as his epilepsy was shown to be the cause of his murderous actions.

In Edwards' case he was sentenced to death, in spite of evidence from all kinds of sources. First, his friend, Mr Marshall, who had seen him arrive early that morning and had observed his pitiable condition; then two medical men insisted that Edwards' case fulfilled the criteria of epilepsy: frequent headaches, moodiness and groundless loss of temper and a history of many such attacks. Of course, there was also no motive at all: he had taken the life of the women he loved and whom he wished to marry.

In court, the jury heard that four years earlier Edwards had wounded another young lady he was courting. He had stabbed her in the arm with his knife, epilepsy had been argued but the plea had been ineffective and for that offence he was given six months' hard labour. Again, Edwards plea of leniency on the grounds of his epilepsy was rejected and the judge placed the black cap on his head to pass sentence of death.

Other witnesses had spoken, such as a Mr Ogden, who said that Edwards had lived with him for a few years and that 'He used to sit in the house with his head in his hands. If asked to move, he would become bad-tempered, get up and bang things about… he would for no reason at all. If asked what was the matter he would make no reply.'

The police surgeon, Dr Rimmer, said that his reading of the homicidal incident was that the man had suffered an epileptic fit. But one witness gave a clear account of a seizure: 'About a year ago I was out with Edwards in a public house. He was quite sober. Suddenly, and without reason, he threw a mug of beer at a man who had just walked past him. I hit Edwards on the side of the jaw. It was not a severe blow, but he turned pale and fell to the ground unconscious. He threw his legs and arms about and it was obvious he was in a fit. Two or three days later I spoke to him about it and he had no recollection of the incident.'

Hitting your friend on the jaw to help seems a strange way to show concern, but at least it produced the kind of evidence that Edwards' counsel must have been looking for. However, it was all to no avail. Even Myrtle's father, at the North Bierley Labour Club, had seen Edwards in a fit and helped to carry him out. He and another man left him in the rain, thinking that would revive him. But the strongest statement came from Edwards' mother, Amy Edwards, who said that he had had two fits when he was just four years old and that he was three years old before he could talk. She said that as he grew older he would have frightening mood-swings and that he tended to fly into a rage if he was disturbed. He had left home in 1934 and lived with his sister, Mrs Ogden, in Lilac Grove Street.

But the most considerable medical statement came from Dr Frederick Eurich of Edinburgh University and a consulting physician at Bradford Royal Infirmary. He said at the trial: 'I have spent three and a half years in a large asylum controlling 2,000 patients, made a special study of mental diseases in England and in Germany… From the facts put before me, I have arrived at the following conclusion, namely that it is highly probable that Edwards suffers from occasional attacks of epilepsy…'

Eurich explained that people like Edwards suffer from loss of memory and waves of depression; he also added that in these states the depression was likely to lead to periodic fits of violence. Apparently, Edwards had lifted Myrtle over a wall after the attack but recalled nothing of that the next day. There had been complete normality earlier on the day of the homicide: Edwards had been at the home of Myrtle's sister, Gladys, and they had both walked to a draper's shop in Tong Street, where Edwards paid for some gloves he had ordered.

Edwards' last statement in court was that for as long as he could remember, he had never felt 'normal in health'. He also stressed that he drank very little alcohol, so that was never a factor in the violence. He was condemned to death, but that was overturned later by the Home Secretary. The campaigner for the abolition of capital punishment, Mrs Van der Elst, wrote in her account of the case: 'I hope Edwards will be given plenty of work to do to keep his mind occupied, so that he can work out his own salvation.' She was one of the unsung heroes of the campaign against hanging, parking her large black car at the gates of prisons on execution day and making a nuisance of herself. Mrs Van der Elst has given us the fullest account of the Edwards case, and her treatment of the facts was exemplary.

WHO KILLED MARY?

UNSOLVED MURDERS ARE TWO-SIDED. THEY LEAVE A PUZZLE FOR POSTERITY, BUT THEY ALSO OFFER NO SATISFACTORY SENSE OF CLOSURE FOR RELATIVES OR FOR POLICE. THE SAD TALE OF A LEEDS WOMAN CUT DOWN IN THE DARK IS ONE SUCH ONGOING 'WHO DUNNIT'.

Mary Judge was well known around the area of Leeds along Kirkgate, between the Parish Church and the Regent Hotel. It is a few streets of dark alleys, not far from the Calls – notoriously unsafe places for walks by night forty years ago. But Mary, forty years old and a cheery, sociable person, liked a drink and liked that area: in many ways a risky business, as may be seen even today, because there is a patch of land (now a small park and well maintained) under the railway arches. The trains above tend to swing around on the viaduct before going on into the station a short way further into the centre of the city.

Mary was discovered at just before midnight by a passer-by on 22 February 1968, battered and with her clothes

Left: The Calls Leeds
– Stanley Walker

Below: The small
park near the railway
arches – The author

scattered around her body. She was only five feet five, with brown hair, and had been wearing quite garish clothes, definitely not colour-coordinated, so that would have made her noticeable. Her skirt was dark blue; the shoes green; a white blouse, and her coat was a black check. She had severe head injuries.

The area was sealed off and arc-lights set up in that dismal, shadowy patch of land. Superintendent Hoban of Leeds CID had barriers erected and asked about her life. She was well known to the barmen of the pubs around there, such as the Brougham, the Regent and other places along Kirkgate. People said she was 'always friendly and happy, liked a drink, and loved to stop and talk to children'. The patch of land is close to the Leeds central bus station, and at that time the area was notorious for its attraction to beggars and tramps, who would often cadge money along the bus station platforms. By day it was busy: there was a huge Pilkington's Glass office nearby, and commuter crowds would walk from the buses, past the abattoir to Vicar Lane. By night, it has to be said, the area was well frequented by prostitutes too. Whether Mary was on the game is not clear, but one interesting point is that she lived in East End Park, on Glendale Street. This was a long walk for her, up towards the Shaftesbury cinema along the York Road. If she was a familiar figure down by the buses, she needed a good reason to walk more than a mile down to the pubs she liked – and alone.

There were witnesses who had seen her being attacked. This was because the Hull train rattled past the Parish Church at eighteen minutes past ten that night, and several people saw the assailant. A small boy was the main witness. He came forward with his mother and gave a description of a tall man of slim build, with long dark hair and wearing a dark suit. Of course, this was February in Yorkshire; but the train passed within a mere fifty yards of the patch of grass where the killing happened. The 8.37 train from Hull would prove to be a key element in the investigation into the heartless slaughter.

Mary had also been seen outside the Regent Hotel in Kirkgate earlier that night, and it soon became obvious that the killer would have had plenty of her blood on his clothes. Appeals were made to local dry-cleaners to be vigilant in inspecting clothes brought in for cleaning in the day after the killing. Nothing came of that, so the train sightings became the main leads.

The Hull train was so important that a reconstruction was staged. Officers boarded a train at Cross Gates, and PC Eileen Playforth took the part of poor Mary Judge. It took just fifteen seconds for the train to pass the scene; it was winter, late at night, and the grass was under the tall arches of the high viaduct. But one positive thing emerged from this: a man was seen leaving the scene by a Bradford man, another passenger on that Hull train. At that point on the train's journey, and passing quite high over the patch of grass, the view would be quite distorted. But there was enough seen to make a helpful descriptive statement.

Of course, readers of true crime stories like an unsolved crime: it opens up the possibility that the reader might come up with a theory. The Judge case is for sure a 'cold case' now but everyone lives in the hope of something turning up. After all, a murder that took place in Halifax in 1957 (again a woman on her own) was thought to be permanently unsolved until a few years ago when Calderdale Police received a phone call referring to a man's death-bed confession.

But of all the unsolved murders in Leeds, this is the one that reaches most deeply into the atmosphere of the Leeds streets in the late sixties. There was something in the air then, a sense of liberation and 'a good time' after the austerities of the decade before. People did socialise more around town, but some areas were 'no go' ones and Mary Judge was surely an easy victim. Her openness to other people would make her very vulnerable. At one time some writers thought that she might have been another 'Ripper' victim but there is no evidence to support this theory. All we are left with is a Leeds mystery.

BIBLIOGRAPHY

Abbot, Geoffrey. - *Lipstick on the Noose* (Summersdale, 2001)

Bland, James. - *True Crime Diary Vol. 2* (Warner Books, 1999)

Campbell, Marie. - *Curious Tales of Old West Yorkshire* (Sigma, 1999)

Clarke A A. - *Killers at Large* (Arton Books, 1996)

Dernley, Syd. with Newman, David. - *The Hangman's Tale* (Pan, 1989)

Eddleston, John J. - *The Encyclopaedia of Executions* (Blake, 2002)

Ellis, John. - *Diary of a Hangman* (True Crime Library, 1997)

Harrison, Paul. - Yorkshire Murders (Countryside Books, 1992)

Jones, Steve. - *Yorkshire- The Sinister Side* (Wicked Books, 2004)

Langan, Paul. - *Valleys of Death* (Breedon Books, 2001)

Rede, Leman Thomas. - *York Castle* (J. Saunders, 1829)

Wade, Stephen. - *Unsolved Yorkshire Murders* (Pen and Sword, 2001)

Watson, Katherine. - *Poisoned Lives: English Poisoners and their Victims* (Hambledon, 2004)

Watson, E R. - *The Trial of Eugene Aram* (William Hodge, 1913)

Whittaker, G H. - *Bill o'Jacks: A Moorland Mystery* (Eclipse Works, 1932)

Wilkinson, George. - *The Newgate Calendar* (Sphere, 1991)

Other books in the Bradwell Books Murder Stories series

AVAILABLE NOW

Leicestershire Murder Stories

Derbyshire Murder Stories

Staffordshire Murder Stories

Nottinghamshire Murder Stories

Lincolnshire Murder Stories

South Wales Murder Stories

Scottish Murder Stories

BRADWELL BOOKS

For more details of these books and other books you may be interested in, visit www.bradwellbooks.com